The CHRISTIAN Lifestyle

A BIBLICAL PERSPECTIVE OF YES OR NO

Jacqueline Hearns

WESTBOW
PRESS

A DIVISION OF THOMAS NELSON

Photograph By: David G. Watkins
Cover Design By: Larry A. Rhodes

Foreword By: Bishop Wayne T. Jackson
Introduction By: Pastor Gerald A. Johnson

WestBow Press books may be ordered through booksellers or by contacting:

WestBow Press
A Division of Thomas Nelson
1663 Liberty Drive
Bloomington, IN 47403
www.westbowpress.com
1-(866) 928-1240

Scripture taken from the Holy Bible, New International Version®. Copyright © 1973, 1978, 1984 Biblica. Used by permission of Zondervan. All rights reserved.

Scripture taken from the King James Version of the Bible.

ISBN: 978-1-4497-6317-6 (sc)
ISBN: 978-1-4497-6318-3 (hbk)
ISBN: 978-1-4497-6316-9 (e)
Library of Congress Control Number: 2012914518

Printed in the United States of America

WestBow Press rev. date: 09/25/2012

In Loving Memory of
My angel
Wanda June Green

Contents

* *All scriptures italicized*
** *All scriptures taken from New International Version unless otherwise noted*
*** *All definitions taken from Wikipedia, The Free Encyclopedia*

Foreword

The *Christian Lifestyle* gives a biblical perspective on making decisions in life. Using examples from her own life, Jacqueline Hearns describes how making the right or the wrong decision can determine an outcome. Readers will learn about the rewards and consequences of their actions. This book is sure to inspire anyone and everyone who reads it.

Bishop Wayne T. Jackson
Sr. Pastor of Impact Ministries Intl'
(Formerly Great Faith Ministries Intl')
Presiding Prelate of Greater Works of Christ Intl' (GWOC)
President and Founder of Impact Network Television Station

Preface

It was Valentine's Day, February 14, 1996, the day my life changed forever; I would never be the same. I was in the ninth grade and had transferred to a new school, so I didn't know anyone other than classmates. My brother had just announced to the *entire* school that I was his sister and if *anybody* tried to "talk" to me, they would have to answer to him. Not many people even looked my way after that. (Thanks, Bro!)

One of my classmates told me his friend liked me and wanted us to meet. He introduced us and his friend gave me a small teddy bear for Valentine's Day. "A teddy bear?" I thought. It was a little corny, but not many people would approach me, thanks to my brother, so I thought it was a little brave also.

By fate we ended up in the same class, working on the same project, so we became good friends. After conversing on the phone, he asked me, "What church do you go to?"

Now the only church I knew was my grandmother's, and it wasn't for me. "I don't go to church," I replied, "but if I ever find one I like, I would go in a heartbeat."

That was an invitation to invite me to his church. Every Sunday his parents would pick me up from home to attend Sunday school and morning worship. (Although they already had multiple children of their own, they somehow had room for one more.) They took me to their home, welcomed me, fed me, loved me, and then took me home. I spent the entire day as "their" child. They became my family outside of my family, and he became my best friend. I didn't know it at the time, but they were raising me to be the child of God He intended me to be. This was our routine every Sunday for at least two years. Then I got my own car and took myself and their older children to church. I was now a part of their family and their church was now my church. I was a part of something bigger than myself, and it felt good. I felt welcomed and at home.

I don't want you to think I didn't have a good life. My life was great. I was raised in a two-parent middle-class home with brothers and sisters, cousins, and friends. My parents did their very best to raise us all to be model citizens. We were protected. I've never been abused, raped, hungry, or left without. I've never missed a holiday feast or even went without an Easter basket with a Cadbury egg. I had a great upbringing. But even with all that, among all those people, I felt alone, and my spirit man was empty. I didn't really have a buddy to occupy me. I had two brothers who were always together. I had two sisters who were always together. My two cousins lived across the street, and they were always together, which left just me. I had to learn to occupy myself. In school, I was always a little different, not like the other children. I didn't want to do what they did, and they didn't want to do what I did. Somehow, I usually ended up by myself. Peer pressure wasn't an issue for me, so I wasn't the child who would do something just to fit in. I didn't have many friends because most kids didn't like me, and most of the time I didn't know why. I had my fair share of problems and consequences, but I was good child so I just couldn't understand why I had so many enemies.

After a while it started to get old so it really didn't matter. I was by myself, with myself, for myself. I began to build a hard shell of protection because no one liked me. The girls hated me, whether I had ever spoken to them or not, the nerds, the fat kids, skinny kids, purple kids—*everybody*. Even the teachers were trying to suspend me without just cause. In creating this hard shell, I also created an attitude: I don't care. I'll be by myself. They don't like me, and I don't like them. Whatever!

I could count my friends on one hand, and that was okay for me. I learned to deal. I had my best friend, who was always there, always around, always available. I finally had someone who I could be with, so it really felt good.

After high school, he moved to another state and left me alone. Here I go again. Life temporarily got a little difficult. He was my "void-filler" and I was his. Whenever or wherever I needed him, he was there and vice versa. I didn't need to depend on anyone else because he was my "everything." But God saw differently. God had to separate us so we both could grow into the people He called us to be, so God could be our everything. It was these years that gave me my "war wounds."

I remember dating a guy in college who was another religion. I was in love with this guy, although I knew it was not a relationship pleasing in God's sight. Every so often I would hear in a whisper, "Why are you with him?" I knew it was God, but I didn't want to hear it. I loved this guy, so I would try to justify the relationship because he loved me back. He filled my "void," and I didn't want to let that go again. I tried to negotiate with God and convince Him that He should allow us to get married. What was I thinking? You can't negotiate with God, the author and finisher of your faith.

I thought God wasn't hearing me. I even tried to use the Word: "You said ask anything in your name, and it shall be given unto me. Why can't I have this?" Looking back, I'm so glad God didn't give me what I wanted. He wasn't my king, he wasn't created for me. God was creating me a man that would be just for me, hand picked. God was creating "my king," but I wasn't ready for him yet. I still had some tears to cry, some pain to endure, some past wounds to heal, and some heartbreaks to overcome. I had some growing up to do within myself.

I had to learn that God will supply all of my needs according to *His* riches in glory (Phil. 4:19), not a man. He couldn't grant my request because it was not according to his riches; it was according to mine. So the request was denied. After years of learning the hard way, we broke up. I was back to square one, alone again.

Then I stepped back and took a good look at myself. I would no longer depend on men, but I would put all my trust, faith, and hope in God and God alone. I would stop looking for a man to fulfill me, and I would seek my fulfillment from God. This was my turning point. I'd had enough. I had cried my last tears, took enough chastisements, and I was tired of being tired. Something had to give, and it was me. I began to live my life according to the Word of God. If the Bible said it, I would do it. If I couldn't find it in the Bible, it had nothing to do with me. It was extreme, but necessary.

God began to place people in my life who would strategically take me closer to my calling. He also showed me myself how others saw me, and it was not a pretty sight. This was the first time I thought I was ugly, when I realized why so many people didn't like me. This was the first time I looked past the "outer me" and saw the "inner me." I had a lot of work to do. It would take more years of pain, tears, changing, rearranging, and overcoming, but this time was different. This time I felt a relationship, that I was special to God. I had finally experienced that love bigger than myself, the love that endures forever. And although I wondered how God could love a sinner like me, He always seemed to reassure me, through His prophets or through a scripture, that I was special in His sight. He truly taught me what Paul meant when he said, "But God demonstrates his own love for us in this: While we were still sinners, Christ died for us." (Rom. 5:8)

Christ died just for me!

Whenever I began to question myself I always found an answer with God. I would love to say that life got easier, but life doesn't get easier when you're looking at yourself. It's easy to point your finger at someone else, but pointing it at yourself becomes a challenge. There were things I did to others that I wouldn't dare allow to happen to me. I didn't realize how mean I was sometimes. And as I learned more about myself, I got harder and harder on myself. I began to despise even looking in the mirror. I thought God had to hate me because He knew everything I did. I would go and do my own thing Monday through Saturday and go to church on Sunday, trying to pretend everything was all right. Who was I kidding? God saw through me and knew exactly what was going on. But it was easier to say I've changed than it was to actually be changed.

Was God trying to tell me that I wasn't going to be perfect? Was He trying to telling me that He still loves me even while I'm sinning? Was He trying to tell me that the Christian lifestyle is a process that wasn't going to change overnight? I just didn't understand. And I can't honestly say I wanted to. I knew I was a bad person, and I was going to hell on a one-way ticket! And just when I thought it was over and I was about to give up, God sent a man, an elder at the church. He prayed for me and told me, "Jackie, you must stop being so hard on yourself. God has already forgiven you. Now it's time to forgive yourself. Jackie, you can't be so hard."

What does that mean? How can you say God has already forgiven me when you don't know what I've been through or what I've done? You don't know the pain I felt! You don't know my story and the heartbreak I've had to overcome! I pondered that for weeks. I knew this man heard from God, so God must have said it. But why to me? How could God forgive me before I forgave myself? So I opened my Bible and asked God for help: "There is therefore now no condemnation to them which are in Christ Jesus, who walk not after the flesh, but after the Spirit" (Rom. 8:1 KJV)

What does this mean? I'm so confused. I need you, God. Help! I cried and cried and cried, but I learned. If God can forgive me, I can forgive myself, so I did. As hard as it was, I had to look at myself and say, "I forgive you." This was the start of a new relationship between Father and daughter, and another new beginning for me.

Since then I have had many "new beginnings," but they all begin the same way: with Christ. Every step I take I ask God to step first, and I won't take one before Him. This book is a new journey for me. During a twenty-one-day fast I heard the Spirit of the Lord say, "I want you to write a book." He began to speak to me, telling me what to say and how to say it.

So often people think that they are the only one's going through something, but they're not. God wanted me to create a book that would scripturally show the positive and negative sides of life and how to deal with them. Each chapter shows the right and wrong way to respond to a situation biblically. It also relates a personal encounter from my life as an example of how I dealt with it, good or bad. And lastly, there are reflection questions so you can think about your life and the decisions you have made in the past. My ultimate goal is that you will think about the reward or consequence before you make the decision and choose to either change your decision and receive the reward or enhance yourself to receive a greater reward.

I pray that this book gives you insight on life and that you obtain wisdom in reading it so that it becomes a stepping stone to greater horizons for you. Of course, there are many more examples and lessons to learn in the Bible. I implore you to find your situation throughout the Bible and turn your test into a testimony.

God Bless!

Jackie

Acknowledgements

~ To my light and source, my heavenly Father, for using me as a scribe and giving me the words to write this book and inspire others. I can never thank you enough!

~ To my wonderful husband and children, who supported me through each and every "bright idea" I had and allowed me to follow through.

~ To my dear mommy for sacrificing all she had so that I could have too.

~ To my family, especially my sister Tajuana, who never judged me, but allowed me to be me and kept me in line when necessary.

~ To Pastors Tony and Alesia Dowdell for opening your home and nurturing me like one of your own.

~To Elder Corey Sanders for mentoring me and planting a desire to get to know God for myself.

~To Pastor Gerald A. Johnson for trusting me to create courses for the youth department, which ultimately led to this book.

~To Bishop Steven and Lady Valorie Bennett for teaching me and building my foundation on a good and solid ground.

~ To Bishop Wayne T. and Dr. Beverly Y. Jackson for speaking into my life and leading me to a higher level in ministry.

~ To anyone who has made an impact in my life to shape me into the woman of God I am today.

~To everyone who believes they're going through something alone and no one understands. You're never alone. God is always there and He understands.

How to use this book

B efore you begin, pray and ask God for an open, receptive heart. This book not only looks at the decisions made by characters in the Bible, it challenges you to look at decisions you've made in the past. Each chapter is broken down into sections:

- **Definition**—Each title word is defined by Wikipedia, The Free Encyclopedia.

- **Personal Encounter**—This autobiographical section looks into the author's personal life. It explores her past experiences, thoughts, emotions, joys, fears, and some of the decisions she made based on the chapter title.

- **Positive Example and Questions**—This section takes an excerpt from the Bible and gives an example of a character who made an acceptable decision, pleasing to God, and describes the rewards resulting from that decision. It then asks some questions based on the excerpt for better clarity and understanding.

- **Negative Example and Questions**—This section looks at the opposite. It takes an excerpt from the Bible and looks at a character who made an unacceptable decision, displeasing to God, and describes the consequences of that decision. It also asks questions based on the excerpt for further clarity and understanding.

- **Self-Reflection**—This section asks open-ended questions and allows you to think about yourself and some of the decisions you have either made or would make if given the opportunity. This is where you examine yourself and determine if you've made the right or wrong decision. You also consider changing your perspective if necessary in hopes of changing the outlook. This may be difficult at first, but it gets easier the more it is practiced.

- **Reference Scriptures**—Scriptures pertaining to each chapter title.

- **Summary**—This section wraps up the topic with some finals thoughts from the author and suggestions to improve negative aspects and become a better person.

After reading this book, you should be able to review a situation beforehand, weigh the pros and cons, make an informed decision, and accept the reward or consequence. This book is sure to make you think before you act.

Introduction

The *Christian Lifestyle* is an awesome teaching manual like no other in the world. One of the most interesting aspects of this book is that it gives you a personal perspective and then challenges you to read and dig deep into the scriptures to find self-application. Jacqueline Hearns has been a student of the Word for many years and actually practices the things contained in this book. *The Christian Lifestyle* is a book that can relate and minister to the needs of those who are teenagers as well as adults. It would be great for a Sunday school session, and it can actually be used in a mid-week Bible study and small-group studies. I recommend this book whole-heartedly, and those who take the challenge and the initiative to complete this God-inspired work will graduate to another level in their walk with God.

Pastor Gerald A. Johnson
Faith Culture Church
Austin, Texas

Chapter One
LIFESTYLE

> ### *Lifestyle (noun)*
> A means of forging a sense of self and to create cultural symbols that resonate with personal identity.

Therefore, if anyone is in Christ, he is a new creation; the old has gone, the new has come! (2 Cor. 5:17)

Personal Encounter

Many "Christians" read the Bible and never apply it to their daily lives. I look back on the lifestyle of my best friend and his family when I first received salvation.

I remember us sitting in class talking. In the midst of our conversation, he proudly said, "I can name all of the books of the Bible in thirty seconds." As he began to recite them, I remember thinking, "That's impressive. I don't know any of them, and he can say them all in thirty seconds." Although I didn't say anything, I was a little embarrassed that I couldn't do the same. Of course, he grew up in the church and spent time studying the Bible and I didn't. But none of that mattered because I couldn't do the same. As I started to spend time with his family, I began to understand why this was so easy for him. His family lived the lifestyle of Christianity inside and outside of the church. Since I spent every Sunday with them, I had the opportunity to observe their lifestyle firsthand and compare it to the Bible.

One thing that turned me away from "church folks" was their attitudes. Monday through Saturday they were just like everybody else. They smoked, drank alcohol, gambled, and hung out after hours in the local nightclub, and their ill-mannered children said every known curse word. But Sunday was totally different. The men had their shiniest patent-leather shoes with the top hat to match. The women had their biggest praise hat with mints in the bottom of their purses, and the entire family were the first ones in church, sitting on the front row, screaming, "Praise the Lord" louder than anyone else. Hypocrites! They were the first to judge and tell you how wrong you were, but they did the same thing. If this was what church was about, I didn't want any part of it. One thing I could appreciate about my family was that they didn't try to live one way on this day and another way on that day. Who they were was who they were, and that was that. They were the same way no matter who was there or what day of the week it was.

As I began to watch my friend's family, I noticed they were the same way in every situation as well. (Looking back, that might have been why I wanted to spend so much time with them. They were just like my family, but from the spiritual perspective. And they had excellent teachers. I had the opportunity to spend personal time with the pastor of the church and his family. They were also the same way in and out of the church. No one put on a front for extra money in the offering, and I appreciated that. All of their children were in church serving. I was truly able to "Experience the love and love the experience," as the church's slogan states.) Their home overflowed with peace and affection; the parents loved one another, and the children respected each other and their parents. It was how a Christian family should be walking in love. They were positive examples. You felt the God in them.

My family wasn't terrible, but we were not living according to the word of God. While I learned valuable lessons like parenting, love, togetherness, and support, they could not teach me the spiritual aspects. However, we were a happy family. We had family game night, when the entire family ate and played games together. We communicated openly to solve disputes. And the water fights in the street were amazing. I have great memories of my childhood, but there was a different energy.

I was blessed with the opportunity to experience firsthand how the Bible says a husband should treat his wife, and how she should reciprocate. I was also able to see how parents should nurture their children so they can grow into the men and women God ordained them to be. I learned from them that being a Christian is not just attending Sunday-morning services, claiming a particular religion, or dressing in the nicest attire; it's a lifestyle. It's about turning from your old way of life, being more Christlike, and becoming a new creature. I am now able to train my children in the way they should go and hopefully when they are older, they will do most of what they learned. I am also able to treat my husband in the way God intended and receive the proper reward. Life isn't always fun, but my joys outweigh my sorrows, so I won't complain. I can proudly say that most of my family is either active members in the church or seeking to know more about God. And although I've been saved for years, I'll never forget what my friend's family did for me. They gave me a gift that no one else could ever give me: an introduction into the welcoming arms of my heavenly Father, a gift that can never be repaid!

Who Pleased God?

After the death of Saul, David returned from defeating the Amalekites and stayed in Ziklag two days. On the third day a man arrived from Saul's camp, with his clothes torn and with dust on his head. When he came to David, he fell to the ground to pay him honor.

"Where have you come from?" David asked him.

He answered, "I have escaped from the Israelite camp."

"What happened?" David asked. "Tell me."

He said, "The men fled from the battle. Many of them fell and died. And Saul and his son Jonathan are dead."

Then David said to the young man who brought him the report, "How do you know that Saul and his son Jonathan are dead?"

"I happened to be on Mount Gilboa," the young man said, "and there was Saul, leaning on his spear, with the chariots and riders almost upon him. When he turned around and saw me, he called out to me, and I said, 'What can I do?'

"He asked me, 'Who are you?'

"'An Amalekite,' I answered.

"Then he said to me, 'Stand over me and kill me! I am in the throes of death, but I'm still alive.'

"So I stood over him and killed him, because I knew that after he had fallen he could not survive. And I took the crown that was on his head and the band on his arm and have brought them here to my lord."

Then David and all the men with him took hold of their clothes and tore them. They mourned and wept and fasted till evening for Saul and his son Jonathan, and for the army of the LORD *and the house of Israel, because they had fallen by the sword.*

David said to the young man who brought him the report, "Where are you from?"

"I am the son of an alien, an Amalekite," he answered.

David asked him, "Why were you not afraid to lift your hand to destroy the LORD's *anointed?"*

Then David called one of his men and said, "Go, strike him down!" So he struck him down, and he died. For David had said to him, "Your blood be on your own head. Your own mouth testified against you when you said, 'I killed the LORD's *anointed.'"* (2 Sam. 1:1-16)

Discussion

1. WHO ARE THE MAIN CHARACTERS?

    David and an Amalekite.

2. WHAT MESSAGE DID THE AMALEKITE RUN TO
    TELL DAVID?

    The Amalekite told David that Saul and his son Jonathan
    had died in battle. He also stated that he was the person
    who killed Saul at his request.

3. WHAT WAS DAVID'S RESPONSE?

    David and all his men tore their clothes and wept and
    fasted until the evening for the death of Saul, his son
    Jonathan, and the army of the Lord who had fallen by
    the sword. He then called one of his men to kill the
    Amalekite to avenge Saul's death.

4. WHY DID DAVID HAVE THE AMALEKITE KILLED?

David had the Amalekite killed to defend Saul's honor. He admitted to David that he killed King Saul, God's anointed, so Saul's blood was on his head.

"Do not touch my anointed ones; do my prophets no harm." *(1 Chron. 16:22)*

5. WHAT WAS DAVID'S REWARD?

David was appointed leader of his people.

After removing Saul, he made David their king. He testified concerning him: 'I have found David son of Jesse a man after my own heart; he will do everything I want him to do.' (Acts 13:22)

6. WHAT CAN WE LEARN FROM DAVID?

We should give honor when honor is due and defend those who can not defend him or herself.

Give everyone what you owe him: If you owe taxes, pay taxes; if revenue, then revenue; if respect, then respect; if honor, then honor. (Rom. 13:7)

Who Displeased God?

K ing Solomon, however, loved many foreign women besides Pharaoh's daughter—Moabites, Ammonites, Edomites, Sidonians and Hittites. They were from nations about which the LORD had told the Israelites, "You must not intermarry with them, because they will surely turn your hearts after their gods." Nevertheless, Solomon held fast to them in love. He had seven hundred wives of royal birth and three hundred concubines, and his wives led him astray. As Solomon grew old, his wives turned his heart after other gods, and his heart was not fully devoted to the LORD his God, as the heart of David his father had been. He followed Ashtoreth the goddess of the Sidonians, and Molech the detestable god of the Ammonites. So Solomon did evil in the eyes of the LORD; he did not follow the LORD completely, as David his father had done.

On a hill east of Jerusalem, Solomon built a high place for Chemosh the detestable god of Moab, and for Molech the detestable god of the Ammonites. He did the same for all his foreign wives, who burned incense and offered sacrifices to their gods.

The LORD became angry with Solomon because his heart had turned away from the LORD, the God of Israel, who had appeared to him twice. Although he had forbidden Solomon to follow other gods, Solomon did not keep the LORD's command. So the LORD said to Solomon, "Since this is your attitude and you have not kept my covenant and my decrees, which I commanded you, I will most certainly tear the kingdom away from you and give it to one of your subordinates. (1 Kings 11:1-11)

Discussion

1. WHO IS THE MAIN CHARACTER?

King Solomon, son of King David.

2. WHY WAS GOD SO ANGRY WITH SOLOMON?

God gave King Solomon more wisdom than any other king before or after him. In King Solomon's latter years, he turned away from God to worship other gods and took many wives. He even collected vast amounts of silver and gold for himself. Even after the warnings, King Solomon did not repent of his sins like his father David.

He must not take many wives, or his heart will be led astray. He must not accumulate large amounts of silver and gold. (Deut. 17:17)

3. HOW MANY WOMEN DID SOLOMON HAVE?

Seven hundred wives and three hundred concubines.

4. WHAT WAS SOLOMON'S CONSEQUENCE?

God tore down his kingdom and gave it to one of his servants.

5. WHAT CAN WE LEARN FROM SOLOMON?

God is the only Supreme God. He is a jealous God. We are to keep Him as Lord and Savior. We must be mindful of putting anything or anyone before God. *Anything* that we honor more than God becomes an idol or a god.

"You shall have no other gods before me. (Ex. 20:3)

6. WHAT STEPS CAN WE TAKE TO CHANGE OUR LIFESTYLE AND BECOME MORE LIKE CHRIST?

a. Confess your sins to God. Truly repent and ask God for forgiveness.

Then I acknowledged my sin to you and did not cover up my iniquity. I said, "I will confess my transgressions to the LORD"--and you forgave the guilt of my sin. Selah (Ps. 32:5)

b. Believe that our Lord and Savior Jesus Christ died on the cross for your sins and that he rose again and is still alive today.

But he was pierced for our transgressions, he was crushed for our iniquities; the punishment that brought us peace was upon him, and by his wounds we are healed. (Isa. 53:5)

c. Receive forgiveness from Jesus Christ and from yourself.

Therefore, there is now no condemnation for those who are in Christ Jesus, because through Christ Jesus the law of the Spirit of life set me free from the law of sin and death. (Romans 8:1-2)

d. Ask for the Lord to come into your life to lead, direct, and order your steps according to His word.

Direct my footsteps according to your word; let no sin rule over me. (Ps. 119:133)

Self-Reflection

1. Have I put away my old self or am I still the same person I was before I was saved?

2. When I'm in church, do I focus more on the Word spoken or on what someone else is wearing?

3. Do I spend more time entertaining others than I do reading my Bible and getting closer to God?

4. Have I been honest with God about my sins and flaws or am I trying to cover them up?

5. Do I understand the meaning behind praise songs or do I just sing along because it sounds good?

6. Do I spend more time on meaningless activities or do I spend more time trying to understand the word of God?

7. Am I trying to lead my life or have I allowed God to be my director?

Reference Scriptures

- But seek first his kingdom and his righteousness, and all these things will be given to you as well. (Matt. 6:33)

- And that in this matter no one should wrong his brother or take advantage of him. The Lord will punish men for all such sins, as we have already told you and warned you. For God did not call us to be impure, but to live a holy life. (1 Thess. 4:6-7)

- Do everything without complaining or arguing, so that you may become blameless and pure, children of God without fault in a crooked and depraved generation, in which you shine like stars in the universe. (Phil. 2:14-15)

Life Application

The world does not stop when you give your life to Christ. There are still journeys to explore and new adventures on which to embark. Life does change, however. There is a transition time during which you will have to remain focused on the end result. Everything we do in life should have a purpose. If it has no purpose, we shouldn't do it. As with anything, a higher level involves another lifestyle change and new lessons to learn. Christianity is not just something we do; it's a lifestyle we live. We are to deny our flesh daily and diligently seek God, putting our "old" selves away, and becoming more like Christ. We all have displeased God at some point in our lives. It's inevitable that we will make mistakes. We are not defined by the mistakes we make but rather by the lessons we learn and overcome and the times we try again. We must remember to truly repent (changing our way of thinking) and ask God for forgiveness, as well as forgive ourselves. We must live the life we preach about, so when people see us, they see Christ and want to be saved also.

Not every day will be your best. There will be times when you want to throw in the towel and give up, but you must stay strong and continue doing what is right. In the end, your blessing will come, and it will be greater than your struggle, and greater than you could even perceive.

Notes

_____

_____

_____

_____

_____

_____

_____

_____

_____

_____

_____

_____

_____

_____

_____

_____

_____

_____

_____

Chapter Two
RESPECT

Respect (noun)
A positive feeling of esteem or deference for a person or other entity.

The tongue has the power of life and death, and those who love it will eat its fruit. (Prov. 18:21)

Personal Encounter

It was the Christmas season 2002. My grandmother invited the entire family to see her perform in a Christmas program at church. I attended her church as a child but had not been there since. While I'm sure it's a great church, it wasn't a great fit for me. I realized that as a child and since my mother did not force me to attend church, I didn't until I found one that was perfect for me.

I was about twenty-one years old at the time, home from college for the Christmas break. I was holding my nephew on my lap while watching my grandmother perform, minding my own business.

Suddenly, an older woman from the church sitting next to me asked, "Is that your son?"

I smiled and replied, "No, this is my nephew."

She frowned and uttered, "Good, cause you're too young to have kids!"

I was so offended. I didn't respond back because my mother taught me to respect my elders, but I felt disrespected. I couldn't pay attention to the rest of the play because I was so frustrated with that "church lady." Not only was I old enough to graduate from college, but in some cultures, I was old enough to have a husband, two children, a house, and a dog. But even though I looked young, who was she to judge and condemn me?

She didn't know anything about me or my life prior to that day. Who was she to tell me whether I was or was not old enough? Was she paying any bills for me? Was she sending me any money that I was unaware of? Was she my mother? She had no significance at all regarding my life. What I was doing with a child was none of her business.

But more importantly, I was in the house of God, a place where love should overflow. The one place where I thought I should be embraced and loved, even if I made a mistake. The one place where my sins should have been forgiven, at least I thought. At this time I was already saved, but if I hadn't been, I would have never returned to church again. I don't believe I ever returned until my grandmother's funeral. Of all places to feel ashamed, church was not one on my list. Church is supposed to be the place of refuge, where you could cast your sins and cares of the world and be refreshed. You should be able to leave in a better place than you were when you came. There should be some sort of joy or peace, contentment when you leave.

The Bible says that we have all fallen short of God's glory, so it's not our place to condemn. It's our place to love and support. It's our place to let the unsaved know that they can find refuge in the church. Jesus told the Pharisees and teachers of the law to cast the first stone if they were without sin. No one could, so why should we?

Situations like this turn our youth away from church and into the streets. All I could think about was a lost sheep staying lost, the many children who have not returned back to church because the person who was supposed to grab them, hug them, and tell them God loves them was the same person who accused them, condemned them, and pushed them away.

Many of our youth will not communicate with adults because they feel condemned or embarrassed by the statements made to them. They feel as if parents don't understand because they have never been through that situation. Many adults do not make this any easier because they act as if they have never been a teenager, and they have no idea what teenagers go through.

Teenagers: Believe it or not, your parents may have been through some of the same things you are going through now and could actually help you out if given the opportunity. Not only that, but some of them have been through and done even more than you have and know first hand of the consequences. They may be trying to prevent you from experiencing what happened to them.

Parents: You don't have to tell them everything, but let them know some things, so they will understand where you are coming from and why you feel how you feel. Don't be embarrassed or ashamed of the decisions you made as a youth. Use that lesson to teach your children so they don't make the same mistake. It may just bring you both closer. I didn't really appreciate why my mother was so strict until my aunt told me some of the things they did as a child. Then I realized that I wasn't so bad and still had time to change and be the best I could be.

Who Showed Respect?

After Saul returned from pursuing the Philistines, he was told, "David is in the Desert of En Gedi." So Saul took three thousand chosen men from all Israel and set out to look for David and his men near the Crags of the Wild Goats.

He came to the sheep pens along the way; a cave was there, and Saul went in to relieve himself. David and his men were far back in the cave. The men said, "This is the day the LORD spoke of when he said to you, 'I will give your enemy into your hands for you to deal with as you wish.'" Then David crept up unnoticed and cut off a corner of Saul's robe.

Afterward, David was conscience-stricken for having cut off a corner of his robe. He said to his men, "The LORD forbid that I should do such a thing to my master, the LORD's anointed, or lift my hand against him; for he is the anointed of the LORD." With these words David rebuked his men and did not allow them to attack Saul. And Saul left the cave and went his way.

Then David went out of the cave and called out to Saul, "My lord the king!" When Saul looked behind him, David bowed down and prostrated himself with his face to the ground. He said to Saul, "Why do you listen when men say, 'David is bent on harming you'? This day you have seen with your own eyes how the LORD delivered you into my hands in the cave. Some urged me to kill you, but I spared you; I said, 'I will not lift my hand against my *master, because he is the LORD's anointed.' See, my father, look at this piece of your robe in my hand! I cut off the corner of your robe but did not kill you. Now understand and recognize that I am not guilty of wrongdoing or rebellion. I have not wronged you, but you are hunting me down to take my life. May the LORD judge between you and me. And may the LORD avenge the wrongs you have done to me, but my hand will not touch you. As the old saying goes, 'From evildoers come evil deeds,' so my hand will not touch you. . . When David finished saying this, Saul asked, "Is that your voice, David my son?" And he wept aloud. "You are more righteous than I," he said. "You have treated me well, but I have treated you badly. You have just now told me of the good you did to me; the LORD delivered me into your hands, but you did not kill me. When a man finds his enemy, does he let him get away unharmed? May the LORD reward you well for the way you treated me today. I know that you will surely be king and that the kingdom of Israel will be established in your hands. (1 Samuel 24: 1-13, 16-20)*

Discussion

1. WHO ARE THE MAIN CHARACTERS?

   David and King Saul.

2. HOW DID DAVID SHOW RESPECT TOWARD SAUL?

   David spared Saul's life. Instead of killing him, he cut the corner of his robe as proof that he could have killed him.

3. WHAT COULD HE HAVE DONE?

   David could have subdued Saul, harmed him, or even killed him without Saul's knowledge.

4. WHY DIDN'T HE?

David did not kill Saul because he was the Lord's anointed.

"Do not touch my anointed ones; do my prophets no harm."
(1 Chron. 16:22)

5. WHAT WAS DAVID'S REWARD?

Saul repented for the way he treated David and told him the kingdom of Israel will be established in his hands.

6. WHAT CAN WE LEARN FROM DAVID?

We should respect those whom God has placed in authority over us, even if they wrong us. It is not our place to repay them; God will handle it in His own way.

Who Did Not Show Respect?

Then he took his staff in his hand, chose five smooth stones from the stream, put them in the pouch of his shepherd's bag and, with his sling in his hand, approached the Philistine.

Meanwhile, the Philistine, with his shield bearer in front of him, kept coming closer to David. He looked David over and saw that he was only a boy, ruddy and handsome, and he despised him. He said to David, "Am I a dog, that you come at me with sticks?" And the Philistine cursed David by his gods. "Come here," he said, "and I'll give your flesh to the birds of the air and the beasts of the field!"

David said to the Philistine, "You come against me with sword and spear and javelin, but I come against you in the name of the LORD Almighty, the God of the armies of Israel, whom you have defied. This day the LORD will hand you over to me, and I'll strike you down and cut off your head. Today I will give the carcasses of the Philistine army to the birds of the air and the beasts of the earth, and the whole world will know that there is a God in Israel. All those gathered here will know that it is not by sword or spear that the LORD saves; for the battle is the LORD's, and he will give all of you into our hands."

As the Philistine moved closer to attack him, David ran quickly toward the battle line to meet him. Reaching into his bag and taking out a stone, he slung it and struck the Philistine on the forehead. The stone sank into his forehead, and he fell facedown on the ground.

So David triumphed over the Philistine with a sling and a stone; without a sword in his hand he struck down the Philistine and killed him.

David ran and stood over him. He took hold of the Philistine's sword and drew it from the scabbard. After he killed him, he cut off his head with the sword. (1 Sam. 17:40-51)

Discussion

1. WHO ARE THE MAIN CHARACTERS?

   David and Goliath.

2. HOW DID GOLIATH DISRESPECT DAVID?

   Goliath judged David based on his size and cursed him
   by his gods. He assumed that David was too small to
   fight him and would be killed in the battle.

3. WHAT WAS DAVID'S RESPONSE?

   David stood firm in what he believed. He told Goliath
   that the Lord will deliver him into his hands, then
   David will kill him, cut his head off, and feed him to
   the animals.

4. WHAT WAS GOLIATH'S CONSEQUENCE?

> David defeated Goliath, cut his head off, and brought it
> to the king and gave glory to the Lord.

> *I have seen something else under the sun: The race is not to*
> *the swift or the battle to the strong, nor does food come to the*
> *wise or wealth to the brilliant or favor to the learned; but time*
> *and chance happen to them all. (Eccl. 9:11)*

5. WHAT CAN WE LEARN FROM DAVID?

> No matter what the circumstances are, as long as the
> Lord is with you, you always have a chance.

6. WHOM SHOULD WE RESPECT?

> A. God—He is a jealous God. We should respect Him with
>   our minds and hearts.

> *"You shall have no other gods before me. (Ex. 20:3)*

> B. Parents—God placed them in our lives to care for us so
>   we should respect them.

> *"Honor your father and your mother, so that you may live long*
> *in the land the LORD your God is giving you. (Ex. 20:12)*

> C. Elders—(an older person).

> *Do not rebuke an older man harshly, but exhort him as if he*
> *were your father. Treat younger men as brothers, older women*
> *as mothers, and younger women as sisters, with absolute purity.*
> *(1 Tim. 5:1-2)*

D. Your neighbor—Everyone.

The entire law is summed up in a single command: "Love your neighbor as yourself." (Gal. 5:14)

E. Yourself—We must learn to respect ourselves before we can truly respect anyone else.

Then God said, "Let us make man in our image, in our likeness, and let them rule over the fish of the sea and the birds of the air, over the livestock, over all the earth, and over all the creatures that move along the ground."

So God created man in his own image, in the image of God he created him; male and female he created them. (Gen. 1:26-27)

Self-Reflection

Think of a time when you *did not* have respect for someone.
1. Who was it?

2. Did he or she do something that went against the Word of God?

3. How did I handle the situation?

4. What could I have done better?

5. How can I prevent the same situation from happening again?

6. Have I learned from this experience, or am I continually repeating the same pattern?

7. Can I mend this situation, or is it best to let it go and learn from it?

8. How can I use this experience as a learning tool for others?

9. What have I done to earn respect? How do I maintain it?

Reference Scriptures

- *Therefore, I urge you, brothers, in view of God's mercy, to offer your bodies as living sacrifices, holy and pleasing to God--this is your spiritual act of worship. (Rom. 12:1)*

- *When they kept on questioning him, he straightened up and said to them, "If any one of you is without sin, let him be the first to throw a stone at her." (John 8:7)*

- *"Honor your father and mother"--which is the first commandment with a promise (Eph. 6:2)*

Life Application

Respect reciprocates. It works both ways. We must demonstrate it in order to receive it, and we must not allow anyone to take it away. We should command respect, not ask and hope we get it, because respect is earned, not given. And we should always carry ourselves in a way that we maintain the respect we've earned.

For example, we should respect the teachers who help us to become better people. Why? Teachers must go through strenuous classes, courses, and training, not only to learn what they know, but also to be able to teach us what they have learned. Because of what they went through, they have earned our respect. The way they carry themselves in the classroom determines the level of respect they receive and whether or not they maintain that level of respect.

The bottom line is: People will only do what you allow. If you allow someone to walk over you, they will. A woman will put on her tallest stilettos and a man his hardest steel toe boots. There is a difference between confidence and arrogance, assertiveness and aggressiveness, submission and gullibility. God never made us to be a doormat for someone to walk over, nor did He make us to dominate anyone either.

We should stand for what we believe and not allow anyone to knock us down. At the same time, we don't have to knock someone else down so that we can stand up. If we all treat others the way we want to be treated, respect would never be an issue.

Notes

_____

_____

_____

_____

_____

_____

_____

_____

_____

_____

_____

_____

_____

_____

_____

_____

_____

❧Chapter Three❧
PEER PRESSURE

Peer Pressure (noun)

The influence exerted by a peer group, encouraging individuals to change their attitudes, values, or behaviors in order to conform to group norms.

Do not conform any longer to the pattern of this world, but be transformed by the renewing of your mind. Then you will be able to test and approve what God's will is—his good, pleasing and perfect will. (Rom. 12:2)

Personal Encounter

As I look back on my life, I cannot think of many times I was pressured into doing anything. My mother raised all of us to have our own minds and not allow anyone to persuade us into doing anything we didn't want to do. (Thanks, Mom!) However, there is one major situation to which I succumbed. I hesitate to even write this because looking back, I just can't believe how one foolish decision affected so many years of my life, causing so many unnecessary emotions. Although I'm not ashamed of the decision I made, I would not want my children to make the same choice. I hope that even as they read this, they learn from my mistake and avoid it.

I remember being in my fourth-grade classroom and listening to my classmates talk about sex. When I was growing up in the 1990s, being a virgin was not a cool thing to be. In fact, you were teased if you even acted like a virgin or if you couldn't join in the conversation. At the time I had not experienced anything sexual, so I would just listen to everyone else's conversation and pretend to understand. (Parents: start talking to your children early about sex. Although you may think they're too young, their classmates do not hesitate to fill in the blanks you avoid. Adolescent children are developing earlier, which sparks the interest of young minds. That interest mixed with television, music, and one experimental ten-year-old could lead to a disaster.)

Since I was not experienced, I began to lie and make up my own stories, although everybody knew I was lying because I'm terrible at it. I wanted to join in the conversation. Years later, I would join the crowd, and I experienced sex far earlier than I should have. So many exciting things were being said that I wanted to experience them for myself. That was a decision that would overtake me for many years to come. Looking back, it wasn't as exciting as they made it out to be, and I definitely should have waited. I am however proud to say that although I was young and made a bad decision, I was very responsible. I practiced safe sex with one person who also had no experience. It was a mutual decision we shared because we cared for each other. Of course the best decision is to wait until marriage to have sex, but at least we were responsible.

For years I tried to break the spirit of fornication but could not. I grew ashamed of myself because I had made such a bad decision that had escalated out of control. Although I was responsible and practiced monogamous safe sex, I still condemned myself for doing something God had strictly forbidden. How could God ever use someone like me? Why is everyone at church smiling at me? Do they know something I didn't tell them? Do they know I'm doing wrong but don't want to say anything? Can they see my sin? How can I stand in front of the younger children and mentor them when I'm doing wrong? What can I say to them? What if I get caught by my pastor? What would he say? What would my parents say if they found out? Why can't I stop when I really want to?

I was so hard on myself. Then one day an elder at the church grabbed me and hugged me. He told me that God loves me and has already forgiven me. It was time to forgive myself. What? What do you mean? How can you say that to someone? How do I forgive myself? How can I move forward once I forgive myself?

It would take years of prayer, pain, and tears to finally forgive myself and overcome this spirit. The Bible tells us that we sometimes do things we know are wrong even when we don't want to do them. It was truly a battle of the spirit against the flesh. I knew it was wrong, and I didn't want to upset God, but I couldn't stop. If only I was strong enough to avoid the situations, maybe it would have helped, but I couldn't even do that. I would tell myself, "This is the last time," but when the situation presented itself again, I did the same thing. I would withhold for a while, but I would always go right back to doing what I knew I wasn't supposed to do. That's how sin is: once you crack the door, the enemy pushes it open, and it's hard to close it again. That's why it's better to just not open the door. I had to finally decide that enough was enough. I had to pray and ask God to deliver me, and I was honest with Him: I couldn't do it myself. No matter how strong I thought I was, I wasn't strong enough to defeat this battle alone. It wasn't until I totally surrendered that I was delivered from the spirit of fornication, and now I am able to help someone else with my testimony.

Who Resisted Peer Pressure?

They said to King Nebuchadnezzar, "O king, live forever! You have issued a decree, O king, that everyone who hears the sound of the horn, flute, zither, lyre, harp, pipes and all kinds of music must fall down and worship the image of gold, and that whoever does not fall down and worship will be thrown into a blazing furnace. But there are some Jews whom you have set over the affairs of the province of Babylon—Shadrach, Meshach and Abednego—who pay no attention to you, O king. They neither serve your gods nor worship the image of gold you have set up."

Furious with rage, Nebuchadnezzar summoned Shadrach, Meshach and Abednego. So these men were brought before the king, and Nebuchadnezzar said to them, "Is it true, Shadrach, Meshach and Abednego, that you do not serve my gods or worship the image of gold I have set up? Now when you hear the sound of the horn, flute, zither, lyre, harp, pipes and all kinds of music, if you are ready to fall down and worship the image I made, very good. But if you do not worship it, you will be thrown immediately into a blazing furnace. Then what god will be able to rescue you from my hand?"

Shadrach, Meshach and Abednego replied to the king, "O Nebuchadnezzar, we do not need to defend ourselves before you in this matter. If we are thrown *into the blazing furnace, the God we serve is able to save us from it, and he will rescue us from your hand, O king. But even if he does not, we want you to know, O king, that we will not serve your gods or worship the image of gold you have set up." Then Nebuchadnezzar was furious with Shadrach, Meshach and Abednego, and his attitude toward them changed. He ordered the furnace heated seven times hotter than usual and commanded some of the strongest soldiers in his army to tie up Shadrach, Meshach and Abednego and throw them into the blazing furnace… Then King Nebuchadnezzar leaped to his feet in amazement and asked his advisers, "Weren't there three men that we tied up and threw into the fire?"*

They replied, "Certainly, O king."

He said, "Look! I see four men walking around in the fire, unbound and unharmed, and the fourth looks like a son of the gods…" Then Nebuchadnezzar said, "Praise be to the God of Shadrach, Meshach and Abednego, who has sent his angel and rescued his servants! They trusted in him and defied the king's command and were willing to give up their lives rather than serve or worship any god except their own God. Therefore I decree that the people of any nation or language who say anything against the God of Shadrach, Meshach and Abednego be cut into pieces and their houses be turned into piles of rubble, for no other god can save in this way." (Dan. 3:9-20, 24-25, 28-29)

Discussion

1. WHO ARE THE MAIN CHARACTERS?

   King Nebuchadnezzar, Shadrach, Meshach, and Abednego.

2. WHAT WAS THE DECREE MADE FOR THE PEOPLE?

   Whenever they hear the sound of instruments, they are to immediately fall down and worship the image of gold. Anyone who resists will be thrown into the blazing fire.

   "You shall have no other gods before me. (Ex. 20:3)

3. WHAT PEER PRESSURE DID THEY EXPERIENCE?

Shadrach, Meshach, and Abednego had to decide if they were going to, like everyone else, serve King Nebuchadnezzar's gods and worship the idol. Or would they resist and continue to worship their God?

"Whoever acknowledges me before men, I will also acknowledge him before my Father in heaven. But whoever disowns me before men, I will disown him before my Father in heaven. (Matt. 10:32-33)

4. HOW DID THEY HANDLE THE SITUATION?

They told the king they were not going to worship his god and that their God would protect them from his hand.

5. WHAT DO YOU THINK WOULD HAVE HAPPENED IF THEY WOULD HAVE WORSHIPPED THE IMAGE?

If they would have worshipped the image of gold, they would not have been harmed by King Nebuchadnezzar. However, God would have been displeased with them, and they may have experienced His wrath.

6. WAS IT WORTH IT FOR THEM?

Absolutely! If we do the will of God, it is always worth the sacrifice. God protects His own. God not only rescued Shadrach, Meshach, and Abednego, but He sent His son to dance with them in the blazing fire.

He said, "Look! I see four men walking around in the fire, unbound and unharmed, and the fourth looks like a son of the gods." (Dan. 3:25)

7. WHAT WAS THEIR REWARD?

God preserved them and rescued them from the burning flames. King Nebuchadnezzar also made a decree that no one could speak against the God of Shadrach, Meshach, and Abednego.

And my God will meet all your needs according to his glorious riches in Christ Jesus. (Phil. 4:19)

8. WHAT CAN WE LEARN FROM THE THREE GENTLEMEN?

Don't allow anyone to pressure you into doing something wrong. Stand up for what you believe in and never deny God, or He will deny you.

Who Gave into Peer Pressure?

The LORD God took the man and put him in the Garden of Eden to work it and take care of it. And the LORD God commanded the man, *"You are free to eat from any tree in the garden; but you must not eat from the tree of the knowledge of good and evil, for when you eat of it you will surely die."* (Gen. 2:15-17)

Now the serpent was more crafty than any of the wild animals the LORD *God had made. He said to the woman, "Did God really say, 'You must not eat from any tree in the garden'?"*

The woman said to the serpent, "We may eat fruit from the trees in the garden, but God did say, 'You must not eat fruit from the tree that is in the middle of the garden, and you must not touch it, or you will die.'"

"You will not surely die," the serpent said to the woman. "For God knows that when you eat of it your eyes will be opened, and you will be like God, knowing good and evil."

When the woman saw that the fruit of the tree was good for food and pleasing to the eye, and also desirable for gaining wisdom, she took some and ate it. She also gave some to her husband, who was with her, and he ate it. . . So the LORD *God said to the serpent, "Because you have done this,*

*"Cursed are you above all the livestock
and all the wild animals!*

You will crawl on your belly
  and you will eat dust
  all the days of your life.
  And I will put enmity
  between you and the woman,
  and between your offspring and hers;
he will crush your head,
  and you will strike his heel."
  To the woman he said,
"I will greatly increase your pains in childbearing;
  with pain you will give birth to children.
Your desire will be for your husband,
  and he will rule over you." (Gen. 3:1-6, 14-19)

Discussion

1. WHO WERE THE MAIN CHARACTERS?

   Eve and the serpent.

2. WHAT WAS GOD'S COMMAND?

   Eat from any tree in the garden, except from the tree of the knowledge of good and evil, or you will die.

3. HOW WAS EVE TEMPTED?

   The serpent, who was the enemy, led Eve to believe that she would not in fact die but that her eyes will be opened and she will be "like" God, knowing good and evil.

   Submit yourselves, then, to God. Resist the devil, and he will flee from you. (James 4:7)

4. WHAT WAS EVE'S RESPONSE?

Eve believed the serpent, in spite of what God commanded. She ate the fruit then gave it to her husband to eat.

5. DID EVE DIE?

Eve did not immediately die a physical death but rather a spiritual death. She and Adam were spiritually separated from God and kicked out of the garden.

But your iniquities have separated you from your God; your sins have hidden his face from you, so that he will not hear. (Isa. 59:2)

6. WHAT WAS THEIR CONSEQUENCE?

They were both kicked out of the garden of Eden and forbidden to return.

Do not be misled: "Bad company corrupts good character." (1 Cor. 15:33)

7. WHAT CAN WE LEARN FROM THIS SITUATION?

Don't question God. God will not tell us to do anything wrong, so we must trust His judgment and obey Him, even when it's not the most popular.

God is not a man, that he should lie, nor a son of man, that he should change his mind. Does he speak and then not act? Does he promise and not fulfill? (Num.23:19)

Self-Reflection

Think of a time you have experienced peer pressure.

1. Did I resist or give in? (How did you solve the situation or problem?)

2. Am I still experiencing it?

3. Was my response pleasing to God? My parents? My friends?

4. What was the reward or consequence? Was it worth it?

5. Could I have just said no? Why or why not?

6. What would have happened if I didn't do this?

7. How can I help someone who may be going through the same thing?

Reference Scriptures

- *In the same way, let your light shine before men, that they may see your good deeds and praise your Father in heaven. (Matt. 5:16)*

- *Watch and pray so that you will not fall into temptation. The spirit is willing, but the body is weak." (Mark 14:38)*

- *It teaches us to say "No" to ungodliness and worldly passions, and to live self-controlled, upright and godly lives in this present age, (Titus 2:12)*

Life Application

Everyone experiences peer pressure at some point in life. It's how you handle the situation that determines the outcome. Every decision you make has either a reward or a consequence attached to it. It's your decision to make, and only you can make it, but you must accept the results. You should never allow anyone to pressure you into something with which you are not comfortable. Ask yourself, "Before I do this, will God be proud of the decision I made, or will He be ashamed?" If the answer is proud, it's a good decision to make. If He will be ashamed, it's a bad decision that you will probably regret.

We must remember as Christians, we are not meant to blend in with worldly things or people. Our old selves are gone, and we have become new, walking in the image of God. We are not supposed to conform to the world; it is supposed to conform to us. In order for that to be possible, we must carry ourselves with high regard, holding to what we believe according to the Word of God.

Notes

_____

_____

_____

_____

_____

_____

_____

_____

_____

_____

_____

_____

_____

_____

_____

_____

_____

_____

_____

_____

ᔆChapter Four᙮
LOVE

Love (noun)
An emotion of a strong affection and personal
attachment. . . the unselfish loyal and benevolent
concern for the good of another". ·

Whoever does not love does not know God, because God is love. (1 John 4:8)

Personal Encounter

Everyone seems to have their own definition of *love*. To some it's a strong feeling. To others it's a secondhand emotion. And yet to someone else, it's a word to say before putting a hand on someone's face.

I remember growing up and seeing my aunt and uncle fight. They would argue and yell profusely. The children always had to go to the next room, but we still could hear. One night their argument escalated into a full blown fight. I want to make this clear: my aunt was no pushover. She was a fighter. She didn't back down to anyone or anything. She said what she meant and stood her ground, but this day was different. It was dark outside, but with the street lights gleaming, you saw everything. They fought like I've never seen them fight before, like they were fighting for the heavyweight championship or something. She left the house and he soon followed chasing after her. He caught her in the middle of the street, grabbed and ripped her shirt causing her to fall and hurt her knee. He dragged her by her shirt into the house and began to slap and punch her all over. She fought back, but he was much bigger and much stronger than her. The cops were called and although no one was arrested, it was a big traumatic deal. I just knew it would be the end of their relationship.

"Why would anyone want to stay in that situation?" I thought. But the next day, we woke to her cooking everyone breakfast, including him.

Not understanding why, I asked, "Why are you still here, I thought you were going to leave him after that?"

She looked me directly in my eyes and said, "We just had a misunderstanding. It's complicated, but he loves me."

I was only about ten years old, but I just couldn't understand why a man would ever put his hands on a woman he loved. Why would they say so many hurtful things to each other if they loved each other? So of course I asked.

"It was just a mix up," she told me. "He apologized, so he won't do that again."

So many questions crossed my mind: How can you be so sure? What if he does? How many times will he hit you before you leave? Will you even get the opportunity to leave? How did it get this far? That very day, I vowed that I never want to be in a relationship with a man who loves me that much!

I was very young and didn't know much, but I knew that being punched was not a good thing, nor was it something I wanted to tolerate. Again, people can only do what you allow them to do. I made up in my mind that I never want to be in a relationship with someone who will physically, emotionally, or mentally abuse me, and in return I would not do those things to another person. I didn't know much about love, but I knew love doesn't cause stitches. Love doesn't embarrass you in front of others. It shouldn't hurt to love; it should feel good. And most important of all, love does not kill, it revives.

Many people loose sight of the true definition (some don't even know the true definition). But the Bible clearly defines exactly what love is, and if it does not line up with the definition according to the Bible, it is not really love. Because God is love, I know that love will not harm me. Love cares for me so much that Love would lay down His life so that I can live. Love would take the bruises so that I don't have to be bruised. Love never fails. Love endures to the end. That's the Love I want.

If someone says he or she loves you but that person's actions don't line up, question that person's definition because, again, love doesn't cause bruises, stitches, or death. You must also be careful of the thin line between love and lust. Sometimes we want love so much that we can make lust look like love, but deep in our heart, we know it's not. If your partner's definition of love includes any form of abuse, leave safely and love from a distance, because that is not the example God has set before us.

If you find it hard to truly love the way God loves, pray. Ask God to teach you how to love like He does. Then expect new revelations and outlooks on life.

Who Displayed Love?

Now two prostitutes came to the king and stood before him. One of them said, "My lord, this woman and I live in the same house. I had a baby while she was there with me. The third day after my child was born, this woman also had a baby. We were alone; there was no one in the house but the two of us.

"During the night this woman's son died because she lay on him. So she got up in the middle of the night and took my son from my side while I your servant was asleep. She put him by her breast and put her dead son by my breast. The next morning, I got up to nurse my son—and he was dead! But when I looked at him closely in the morning light, I saw that it wasn't the son I had borne."

The other woman said, "No! The living one is my son; the dead one is yours."

But the first one insisted, "No! The dead one is yours; the living one is mine." And so they argued before the king.

The king said, "This one says, 'My son is alive and your son is dead,' while that one says, 'No! Your son is dead and mine is alive.'"

Then the king said, "Bring me a sword." So they brought a sword for the king. He then gave an order: "Cut the living child in two and give half to one and half to the other."

The woman whose son was alive was filled with compassion for her son and said to the king, "Please, my lord, give her the living baby! Don't kill him!"

But the other said, "Neither I nor you shall have him. Cut him in two!"

Then the king gave his ruling: "Give the living baby to the first woman. Do not kill him; she is his mother."

When all Israel heard the verdict the king had given, they held the king in awe, because they saw that he had wisdom from God to administer justice. (1 Kings 3:16-28)

Discussion

1. WHO ARE THE MAIN CHARACTERS?

   Two scarlet women, (one considered a "mother," the other "a woman") and King Solomon.

2. WHAT WAS THE WOMEN'S DISAGREEMENT?

   The women were debating whose son was the living son, both claiming he was theirs. However, the woman's child died because his mother laid on him while sleeping.

3. WHAT WAS KING SOLOMON'S SOLUTION?

Cut the living child in half and give one half of the child to each woman. That way, both could share the child. This solution proved him to be the wisest of all men.

Solomon's wisdom was greater than the wisdom of all the men of the East, and greater than all the wisdom of Egypt. (1 Kings 4:30)

4. WHAT WAS THE WOMAN'S RESPONSE?

The woman agreed with King Solomon. She figured since her child had died, no one else should have a child.

5. WHAT WAS THE MOTHER'S RESPONSE?

The mother could not bear to see her child killed and would rather give the child to the woman unharmed. The mother told King Solomon to give the child to the woman so that the child would not be killed.

6. WHAT WAS THE MOTHER'S REWARD?

The mother was able to keep her child, while the woman no longer had a child.

7.   WHAT CAN WE LEARN FROM THE WOMEN?

There is a difference between a mother and a woman who has a child. Mothers have unconditional love and would rather sacrifice themselves than see their child harmed. They want the best for their child, even when the child does not reciprocate. Women who had children have no regard for the life they bore, no connection, and therefore no relationship. The priority of the child is less than their own.

But God demonstrates his own love for us in this: While we were still sinners, Christ died for us. (Rom. 5:8)

Who Did Not Display Love?

In the course of time, Amnon son of David fell in love with Tamar, the beautiful sister of Absalom son of David.

Amnon became frustrated to the point of illness on account of his sister Tamar, for she was a virgin, and it seemed impossible for him to do anything to her. . .

So Tamar went to the house of her brother Amnon, who was lying down. She took some dough, kneaded it, made the bread in his sight and baked it. Then she took the pan and served him the bread, but he refused to eat.

"Send everyone out of here," Amnon said. So everyone left him. Then Amnon said to Tamar, "Bring the food here into my bedroom so I may eat from your hand." And Tamar took the bread she had prepared and brought it to her brother Amnon in his bedroom. But when she took it to him to eat, he grabbed her and said, "Come to bed with me, my sister."

"Don't, my brother!" she said to him. "Don't force me. Such a thing should not be done in Israel! Don't do this wicked thing. What about me? Where could I get rid of my disgrace? And what about you? You would be like one of the wicked fools in Israel. Please speak to the king; he will not keep me from being married to you." But he refused to listen to her, and since he was stronger than she, he raped her.

Then Amnon hated her with intense hatred. In fact, he hated her more than he had loved her. Amnon said to her, "Get up and get out!"

. . . But Jonadab son of Shimeah, David's brother, said, "My lord should not think that they killed all the princes; only Amnon is dead. This has been Absalom's expressed intention ever since the day Amnon raped his sister Tamar. (2 Sam. 13:1-2, 8-15, 32)

Discussion

1. WHO ARE THE MAIN CHARACTERS?

    Amnon and Tamar, children of King David.

2. WHAT DID AMNON ASK OF HIS SISTER?

    He "loved" her so much that it made him sick. So he asked her to come and lay with him.

3. HOW DID SHE RESPOND?

    She told him it was a disgrace to commit sexual immorality before marriage. She asked him to speak to their father, the king, who will give them permission to marry.

    Flee from sexual immorality. All other sins a man commits are outside his body, but he who sins sexually sins against his own body. (1 Cor. 6:18)

4. WHAT WAS AMNON'S REACTION TO TAMAR?

Because he was stronger, he forced himself on her and raped her, then kicked her out of his room.

It is God's will that you should be sanctified: that you should avoid sexual immorality; that each of you should learn to control his own body in a way that is holy and honorable, not in passionate lust like the heathen, who do not know God; (1 Thess. 4:3-5)

5. WHAT WAS AMNON'S CONSEQUENCE?

Amnon was eventually killed by his brother Absalom.

"'If a man marries his sister, the daughter of either his father or his mother, and they have sexual relations, it is a disgrace. They must be cut off before the eyes of their people. He has dishonored his sister and will be held responsible. (Lev. 20:17)

6. WHAT CAN WE LEARN FROM THIS SITUATION?

People view love differently. We must all be able to define love for ourselves or others will try to define it for us. But love does not hurt.

7. HOW DOES THE BIBLE DEFINE LOVE?

Love is patient, love is kind. It does not envy, it does not boast, it is not proud. It is not rude, it is not self-seeking, it is not easily angered, it keeps no record of wrongs. Love does not delight in evil but rejoices with the truth. It always protects, always trusts, always hopes, always perseveres. (1 Cor. 13:4-7)

8. WHAT ARE SOME WAYS CAN WE SHOW LOVE?

   a. Represent God by walking in the love He gave you.

      Be imitators of God, therefore, as dearly loved children and live a life of love, just as Christ loved us and gave himself up for us as a fragrant offering and sacrifice to God. (Eph. 5:1-2)

   b. Understand that God is love.

      Dear friends, let us love one another, for love comes from God. Everyone who loves has been born of God and knows God. Whoever does not love does not know God, because God is love. (1 John 4:7-8)

   c. Love everyone, even those who persecute you.

      Therefore, as God's chosen people, holy and dearly loved, clothe yourselves with compassion, kindness, humility, gentleness and patience. Bear with each other and forgive whatever grievances you may have against one another. Forgive as the Lord forgave you. (Col. 3:12-13)

   d. Don't just talk about, be about it.

      Dear children, let us not love with words or tongue but with actions and in truth. (1 John 3:18)

e. Love the things of God and the will of God more than the world.

Do not love the world or anything in the world. If anyone loves the world, the love of the Father is not in him. For everything in the world—the cravings of sinful man, the lust of his eyes and the boasting of what he has and does—comes not from the Father but from the world. The world and its desires pass away, but the man who does the will of God lives forever. (1 John 2:15-17)

Self-Reflection

1. How do I define love and does it agree with how God defines love?

2. Have I forgiven those who have harmed me or am I harboring the hurt inside?

3. How can I show others that I love them? What can I do for them?

4. Can I make a difference in someone's life by showing them love? If so, how?

5. Do I love others because they love me, or do I love even if I don't receive the same response back?

6. When I say, "I love you," is it genuine, or do I have an ulterior motive?

7. How do other people perceive my love?

Reference Scriptures

- "For God so loved the world that he gave his one and only Son, that whoever believes in him shall not perish but have eternal life. (John 3:16)

- "If you love those who love you, what credit is that to you? Even 'sinners' love those who love them. (Luke 6:32)

- If anyone says, "I love God," yet hates his brother, he is a liar. For anyone who does not love his brother, whom he has seen, cannot love God, whom he has not seen. (1 John 4:20)

Life Application

There is no love greater than one who would give his or her life for someone else. God loved us so much He gave His son Jesus, who willingly gave His life for us. How marvelous is that? Even when people turned their backs on Him, He still said, "I love you." Even when they denied Him and His word, He still said, "I love you." Even when the same people who praised Him, persecuted and crucified Him, He asked God to forgive them and still loved them. What a great example. Nothing can ever surpass that. And we as His children must aspire to do the same.

We should love everyone, not just those who love us in return. Love is truly an action word. It has the power to break down and the power to lift up, so we must be mindful when we use it. We may not always be happy about what a person has done to us, but we must still love them because our Father loves us. And before we can love anyone else, we must love ourselves. We must be able to look ourselves in the mirror and ask, "What's good *and* bad about me?" "What are my strengths *and* weaknesses?" "Am I willing to accept these things or change?"

Once you are willing to accept yourself for who you are, you can love yourself the way you are. Then you can then truly love someone else in return.

Notes

_____

_____

_____

_____

_____

_____

_____

_____

_____

_____

_____

_____

_____

_____

_____

_____

_____

_____

_____

_____

_____

_____

∽Chapter Five∾
GIVING

Giving (verb)
The transfer of something without the expectation of payment.

Give, and it shall be given unto you; good measure, pressed down, and shaken together, and running over, shall men give into your bosom. For with the same measure that ye mete withal it shall be measured to you again. (Luke 6:38 KJV)

Personal Encounter

I love to give! Even as a child, I'd give the shirt off my back if someone needed it. But why is it that people always have something to say when you're giving to the church? I remember when I was first saved, everybody had something to say about giving. "Why are you giving all your money to the church? All you're doing is paying for the pastor's lifestyle? Why should you have to give 10 percent of your check? You worked for it, not them?" "I don't go to church because I don't want to give my money, etc." I tried to ignore them all until one day my pastor gave an unorthodox sermon on giving which made me question everything. I was expecting the usual, "You must give your tithes and offering so God will bless you." But this day was different.

Pastor Steven J. Bennett, Sr. of House of Prayer and Praise Ministries in Detroit, grabbed the mic and said, "God don't need your money and neither do I. If you don't give, God will be okay and so will I.

God will bring others who will give and they don't have to be forced. His house will be taken care of and so will mine because I serve Him with a pure heart. The lights and heat were working before you came to the church, and they will work if you leave. We'll miss you, but we will be all right because God is with us."

I had never heard a message like that. I didn't know if I should have been appreciative because of his honesty or upset because of his honesty. I just didn't know how to take that kind of honesty. For a couple of days I sat and thought about what he said. What was he trying to imply? Should I be offended? Was that meant for me? Why am I giving in the first place? I didn't go to church all the time, but I knew that giving was an important part of the service. But I still couldn't answer my questions. So I decided to test the message. For the entire summer I didn't give at all—no tithes, no offering, no special seed, nothing. I wanted to see if the message was true, if my giving was really necessary for me. And I noticed that the lights still worked, the air conditioning was intact, and the pastor still smiled at everyone. It was church as usual. It didn't skip a beat. But I was different. Suddenly, my hours were cut at work, so I made less money. I also didn't feel my normal self. Giving became a burden because I didn't have it to give. Sometimes it was a little embarrassing because I couldn't do things I was able to do in the past. I felt like I went backward. Life was a little harder for me. It was weird. Maybe it was just me, but I knew it concerned withholding my offerings from the church. So I started to give again, and I could see the difference in my life.

I learned a valuable lesson that summer, one I would never forget: when I'm stingy with God, God is stingy with me. I never again want to be in a place where God holds back what He has for me. I want everything He has for me.

I also adopted a new analogy: a gift to others is a gift to me. What do I mean by that? In order for me to give to others, I must first have it myself. The more I have, the more I can give.

So many people miss their blessing because of their stingy attitudes. I believe they totally missed the fact that God doesn't need us, we need Him. When we give we should give willingly and with a pure heart. Only then will God accept our offering. Otherwise, it becomes "stink" to God, an unacceptable gift with no blessing attached. That is usually the time when someone else receives the blessing that was supposed to be attached to your giving. And what's interesting is when someone receives your blessing, not only do you know that you did *not* receive it, but you also know who has it and you can see *your* blessing on them. It's just not worth missing your blessing!

Who Gave with a Pure Heart?

S ome time later the brook dried up because there had been no rain in the land. Then the word of the LORD came to him: "Go at once to Zarephath of Sidon and stay there. I have commanded a widow in that place to supply you with food." So he went to Zarephath. When he came to the town gate, a widow was there gathering sticks. He called to her and asked, "Would you bring me a little water in a jar so I may have a drink?" As she was going to get it, he called, "And bring me, please, a piece of bread."

"As surely as the LORD your God lives," she replied, "I don't have any bread—only a handful of flour in a jar and a little oil in a jug. I am gathering a few sticks to take home and make a meal for myself and my son, that we may eat it—and die."

Elijah said to her, "Don't be afraid. Go home and do as you have said. But first make a small cake of bread for me from what you have and bring it to me, and then make something for yourself and your son. For this is what the LORD, the God of Israel, says: 'The jar of flour will not be used up and the jug of oil will not run dry until the day the LORD gives rain on the land.'"

She went away and did as Elijah had told her. So there was food every day for Elijah and for the woman and her family. For the jar of flour was not used up and the jug of oil did not run dry, in keeping with the word of the LORD spoken by Elijah. (1 Kings 17:7-16)

Discussion

1. WHO ARE THE MAIN CHARACTERS?

    Elijah the prophet and the widow woman at Zarephath.

2. WHAT WAS THE WIDOW WOMAN ASKED TO DO?

    She was asked to first make Elijah the prophet a small loaf of bread and bring him water to drink, and then make food for herself and son.

3. WHAT WAS HER RESPONSE?

    She stated that she only had one meal left, enough for the two of them to have and then die.

4. WHAT DID SHE GIVE?

> She did as the prophet told her: she made a meal for him
> first, then for the two of them.

5. WHAT WAS HER REWARD?

> There was food for the three of them every day, just as
> Prophet Elijah said. It did not run out.
>
> *One man gives freely, yet gains even more; another withholds
> unduly, but comes to poverty. (Prov. 11:24)*

6. WHAT CAN WE LEARN FROM THIS SITUATION?

> Giving is not about the size, it's about the sacrifice and
> the heart in which it was given.
>
> *A generous man will prosper; he who refreshes others will
> himself be refreshed. (Prov. 11:25)*

Who Gave with a Deceitful Heart?

Now a man named Ananias, together with his wife Sapphira, also sold a piece of property. With his wife's full knowledge he kept back part of the money for himself, but brought the rest and put it at the apostles' feet.

Then Peter said, "Ananias, how is it that Satan has so filled your heart that you have lied to the Holy Spirit and have kept for yourself some of the money you received for the land? Didn't it belong to you before it was sold? And after it was sold, wasn't the money at your disposal? What made you think of doing such a thing? You have not lied to men but to God."

When Ananias heard this, he fell down and died. And great fear seized all who heard what had happened. Then the young men came forward, wrapped up his body, and carried him out and buried him.

About three hours later his wife came in, not knowing what had happened. Peter asked her, "Tell me, is this the price you and Ananias got for the land?"

"Yes," she said, "that is the price."

Peter said to her, "How could you agree to test the Spirit of the Lord? Look! The feet of the men who buried your husband are at the door, and they will carry you out also."

At that moment she fell down at his feet and died. Then the young men came in and, finding her dead, carried her out and buried her beside her husband. Great fear seized the whole church and all who heard about these events. (Acts 5:1-11)

Discussion

1. WHO ARE THE MAIN CHARACTERS?

   Annanias and Sapphira, husband and wife.

2. WHAT WERE THEY SUPPOSED TO DO?

   They were supposed to sell all of their property and place all of the profits at the apostle's feet.

   All the believers were one in heart and mind. No one claimed that any of his possessions was his own, but they shared everything they had. (Acts 4:32)

3. WHAT DID THEY DO INSTEAD?

   They kept a portion of the money for themselves and placed the rest at the apostle's feet. Sapphira later lied and said they gave the full price knowing that they did not.

   For where your treasure is, there your heart will be also. (Matt. 6:21)

4. WHAT WAS THEIR CONSEQUENCE?

Both dropped dead where they were standing for testing the Holy Spirit.

For the wages of sin is death, but the gift of God is eternal life in Christ Jesus our Lord. (Rom. 6:23)

5. WHY WAS WITHHOLDING FROM THE HOLY SPIRIT PUNISHABLE BY DEATH?

It was more than that they just withheld their offering from the Holy Spirit. Under the influence of Satan, not only did they withhold the funds, but they tried to deceive Peter and the Holy Spirit by lying and selfishly keeping part of the profits, among other things. Their hearts were wrong.

Death and Destruction lie open before the LORD--how much more the hearts of men! (Prov. 15:11)

6. WHAT ARE SOME PRINCIPLES TO GIVING?

a. Take care of God's house.

Bring the whole tithe into the storehouse, that there may be food in my house. Test me in this," says the LORD Almighty, "and see if I will not throw open the floodgates of heaven and pour out so much blessing that you will not have room enough for it. (Mal. 3:10)

b. Give not to be seen.

But when you give to the needy, do not let your left hand know what your right hand is doing, so that your giving may be in secret. Then your Father, who sees what is done in secret, will reward you. (Matt. 6:3-4)

c. Give with a pure heart.

Remember this: Whoever sows sparingly will also reap sparingly, and whoever sows generously will also reap generously. Each man should give what he has decided in his heart to give, not reluctantly or under compulsion, for God loves a cheerful giver. (2 Cor. 9:6-7)

d. Give with a clean heart.

"Therefore, if you are offering your gift at the altar and there remember that your brother has something against you, leave your gift there in front of the altar. First go and be reconciled to your brother; then come and offer your gift. (Matt. 5:23-24)

e. Give not expecting anything in return.

In everything I did, I showed you that by this kind of hard work we must help the weak, remembering the words the Lord Jesus himself said: 'It is more blessed to give than to receive.'"(Acts 20:35)

f. Give willingly.

The LORD said to Moses, "Tell the Israelites to bring me an offering. You are to receive the offering for me from each man whose heart prompts him to give. (Ex. 25:1-2)

g. Receive the blessing God gives you.

The blessing of the LORD brings wealth, and he adds no trouble to it. (Prov. 10:22)

7. BESIDES GIVING MONEY, WHAT ELSE DOES GOD WANT US TO GIVE? AND HOW?

a. Time—Serving and assisting in the ministry where needed.

b. Talents—Working in the ministry.

c. Loyalty—Supporting and praying for the leaders.

d. Prayers—Praying without ceasing.

Do not be deceived: God cannot be mocked. A man reaps what he sows. (Gal. 6:7)

Self-Reflection

1. To whom am I giving to? Have I considered the receiver?

2. Is this my best? Can I give more without hurting myself?

3. Am I giving with a pure heart?

4. Am I giving to be seen by others or by no one at all?

5. How do I feel as a giver? How might the receiver feel?

6. Is my giving acceptable to God?

7. If I am giving to God, will this help to spread the gospel of Jesus Christ?

8. How did the receiver receive my gift? What was his or her response?

9. What am I giving to glorify God? (offerings, time, talents, etc.)

Reference Scriptures

- *The good man brings good things out of the good stored up in his heart, and the evil man brings evil things out of the evil stored up in his heart. For out of the overflow of his heart his mouth speaks. (Luke 6:45)*

- *If you, then, though you are evil, know how to give good gifts to your children, how much more will your Father in heaven give good gifts to those who ask him! (Matt. 7:11)*

- *"Be careful not to do your 'acts of righteousness' before men, to be seen by them. If you do, you will have no reward from your Father in heaven. (Matt. 6:1)*

Life Application

Some people are looking for God to stop the earth from spinning, get off the throne, put on His cloak of many colors, put the mantle on His shoulders, walk through the heavenly white gates, go down the stairs, and knock on their personal door. In the twinkling of an eye, he or she would open it, then God Almighty would personally hand that person a check for ten million dollars and say, "I love you. Bless you my child." Well, good luck. Not gonna happen!

God doesn't work like that, and if you're waiting for that to happen, don't hold your breath. God allows or causes "man" to give. Who is man? Man could come in the form of a pay raise, your neighbor may feel the unction to pay your light bill next month, or a total stranger may feel led to pay off your entire mortgage. Many people miss their blessing because they are only looking for it to come a certain way. We never know how our blessing will come, so we must always be in a mode of expectation, and while we are waiting, we must bless someone else.

Give because you want to, not because you have to. And give cheerfully. Only then will it and you be blessed.

Notes

_____

_____

_____

_____

_____

_____

_____

_____

_____

_____

_____

_____

_____

_____

_____

_____

_____

_____

ᵰ Chapter Six ᵱ
FAITH

Faith (noun)

Belief in a god or gods or in the doctrines
or teachings of the religion. Trust or belief
without proof.

Now faith is the substance of things hoped for, the evidence of things not seen.
(Heb. 11:1 KJV)

Personal Encounter

Faith has its own special way of working out even far beyond what you can ever imagine or dream. If I never had anything in life, I at least had faith.

When I was about nineteen years old and in college, I sat on my bed in the dorm to have a conversation with God. Now many people think that at nineteen, one could not have gone through much in relationships, but I beg to differ. By the age of nineteen, I was done with the dating game and the entire male species! I had more than my share of "B's"—the want to-be, could-be, would never-be, trying to be, used to be, don't know how to be, and everyone else in between. I had had so many pains, tears, and heartaches, I couldn't bare one more.

So I prayed to God, and all I could say was, "Help, Father. I need you!" I asked God for someone special, my husband, the one who was created just for me. I told myself, "God told Habakkuk to write the vision and make it plain. So if he could do it, so could I."

I wrote down my vision of what I wanted my husband to be and I made it plain. I asked God specifically for the husband I wanted Him to create for me. From the top of his head to the soles of his feet, I wrote in detail. I asked, I really asked. Looking back, I know God had to laugh because some of the things were just plain funny. For instance, I asked, "God, will you make his toes curve evenly so that when I look at them, they are pretty? And will you make his nose proportioned to his face, so when I look at him, I don't just see it? And, God, please let his last name by one syllable because my first name is long enough. And God, can he be a…"

One of my weirdest requests was: "God let this man be someone I've already known before but never dated." That way I knew he would like me for me and nothing else. I went on for hours about how I wanted this man to be, inside and out. I described his hair, height, eyes, hobbies, likes, dislikes, emotions, strengths, weaknesses, family, everything. I even asked God to not just make him a man of God, but that he would live according to the Word of God. I just knew this man would be something special, one of a kind, a man like no other.

My last prayer was: "God will you send him to me after I graduate college so I can concentrate on my studies, and will you change me into the wife that he wants me to be?"

Of all things to pray for, I asked to change me, not him (If I would have only known what I prayed for I might have asked differently). I knew this guy would be something special, so I didn't mind changing because I wanted us to be happy.

I was honest with myself. I was not ready for marriage at that time nor was I marriage material. I had a lot of work to do, and I didn't want to do it all myself. I knew God was going to have to help me or it wouldn't get done correctly.

Sometimes how we see ourselves is not always how God sees us. We think we have it all together when we are really a mess. I knew I was a mess, but I wanted my husband to see me how God sees me, and the only way that could be done was if I allowed God to change me into the wife He wanted me to be. I couldn't do that.

During the course of four years (it took a while, God had a lot of work to do!) God operated on me. He stood me in front of the mirror and showed me myself. Some of it was not a pretty sight. When God shows you yourself, occasionally it's hard to look at because you may not always want to see what's there. Sometimes there are things in us passed down from generations that we may not have even recognized. And sometimes there are hurts in us that we don't want to rekindle or anger we don't want to address. So the operation began.

I understood that before I could ask God to change someone else, I must first ask Him to change me. God revealed things that I never knew were there. There were heartaches of the past that I had not gotten over. I could have never totally given myself to anyone nor could I have fully satisfied my husband the way he was supposed to be satisfied. I couldn't fully satisfy myself either. There were many days and nights of praying and crying, wondering why I had to go through so much transformation. Was he that special? I even got to the point of telling God if my husband didn't like who I was now, he just won't like me. It was at that point God brought back to my remembrance that I asked for it, so I had to deal with whatever He saw fit. It was a hurtful realization at the time, but looking back it was well worth it, because now I am whole and free from my past. I can love my husband the way he deserves to be loved. More importantly, I can love myself the way I deserve to be loved.

During this four-year transformation I encountered many doubts, fears, and objections. As I began to tell people about my incredible husband, they would tell me my standards were too high, no guy could ever reach them. I even had one guy tell me, "The only guy who fits that description is Jesus, and you can't marry Him!"

At some point I started to question myself. Was I setting the standard too high? Should I lower it to have more candidates? Will I be single all my life if no one measures up? Did I ask God for too much? The devil even came and asked, "If this guy is so great, wouldn't you have dated him before?"

Now this question got me. You're right. He sounds amazing; maybe he doesn't exist. But then I began to speak life into my situation. (Sometimes if there is no one else to speak into your situation, you must speak into your own situation.) And so I did.

"My father told me to ask anything in His name and believe and He'll give it to me. He said to write the vision and make it plain, and that's what I did. I'm only looking for the *one* man whose rub I carry; I don't need a lot of candidates. The only thing I need is for God to reveal him to me when he comes."

And so I waited. I had already shed my last tear, so I wasn't going to cry during this process. Every now and then God allows us to go through the fire so He can see what we are really made of. I believe God wanted to see if I really put my trust in Him or if I was just talking. I told myself I was going to wait as long as I had to because I was not going to marry until God revealed to me my husband and I knew for sure.

Finally, the time had come, just as I prayed, one month after I graduated from college. I met my husband, and he was exactly how I described him from the top of his head to the soles of his feet. God had revealed to me his silhouette many times in my dreams, so I knew he existed and that I would recognize him whenever I saw him. That's one of the reasons I love God so much. In the midst of our trials when we are going through the process, He always gives us something to let us know He's still with us. Something to hold onto, and that's what I needed in the wilderness.

When God revealed my husband to me, I couldn't believe it. I had prayed so long and thanked Him so much that when the day came I didn't know what to do. It's so funny that sometimes we pray for things and then when God gives them to us, we don't know how to react. I must have asked God twenty times if this was the man I had prayed for, just to be sure. I think I asked God so much that He told me not to ask Him again.

So on our first date, I was overjoyed. I told him that he was my husband and that he was going to marry me the next year. I was so sure by now he was the one, I even told him the date we'd be married: August 6. I was confident that what I was saying would come to pass. He, of course, was not. He laughed. This was our first date. He had no plans of marriage and thought, "What's wrong with this girl, I'm never getting married." He didn't know I had prayed for a long time for this meeting. We dated for a couple of months and he proposed. Yes, he proposed. It was everything I wanted it to be and more. On August 6 the next year, I put the deposit down on our hall. A couple of months later we married, just as I had asked in my college dorm room at nineteen. God works in mysterious ways.

Who Displayed Faith?

A s he went along, he saw a man blind from birth. His disciples asked him, "Rabbi, who sinned, this man or his parents, that he was born blind?"

"Neither this man nor his parents sinned," said Jesus, "but this happened so that the work of God might be displayed in his life. . .

Having said this, he spit on the ground, made some mud with the saliva, and put it on the man's eyes. "Go," he told him, "wash in the Pool of Siloam" (this word means Sent). So the man went and washed, and came home seeing.

His neighbors and those who had formerly seen him begging asked, "Isn't this the same man who used to sit and beg?" Some claimed that he was.

Others said, "No, he only looks like him."

But he himself insisted, "I am the man."

"How then were your eyes opened?" they demanded.

He replied, "The man they call Jesus made some mud and put it on my eyes. He told me to go to Siloam and wash. So I went and washed, and then I could see."

"Where is this man?" they asked him.

"I don't know," he said.

They brought to the Pharisees the man who had been blind. Now the day on which Jesus had made the mud and opened the man's eyes was a Sabbath.

Therefore the Pharisees also asked him how he had received his sight. "He put mud on my eyes," the man replied, "and I washed, and now I see."

Some of the Pharisees said, "This man is not from God, for he does not keep the Sabbath."

But others asked, "How can a sinner do such miraculous signs?" So they were divided. . .

A second time they summoned the man who had been blind. "Give glory to God," they said. "We know this man is a sinner."

He replied, "Whether he is a sinner or not, I don't know. One thing I do know. I was blind but now I see!" (John 9:1-3, 6-16, 24-25)

Discussion

1. WHO IS THE MAIN CHARACTER?

   Jesus and a man born blind.

2. WHAT WAS HIS DILEMMA?

   From birth he was unable to see.

3. WHAT HAPPENED?

   Jesus spit on the ground to make mud. He then covered the man's eyes and told him to go to the Pool of Siloam and wash.

4. WHAT WAS HIS REWARD?

   The man went and washed and was able to see.

   In the same way, faith by itself, if it is not accompanied by action, is dead. (James 2:17)

5. WHAT CAN WE LEARN FROM THIS SITUATION?

If you believe in your heart and follow God's command, nothing is impossible, regardless of what anyone says.

"'If you can'?" said Jesus. "Everything is possible for him who believes." (Mark 9:23)

Who Lacked Faith?

Immediately Jesus made the disciples get into the boat and go on ahead of him to the other side, while he dismissed the crowd. After he had dismissed them, he went up on a mountainside by himself to pray. When evening came, he was there alone, but the boat was already a considerable distance from land, buffeted by the waves because the wind was against it.

During the fourth watch of the night Jesus went out to them, walking on the lake. When the disciples saw him walking on the lake, they were terrified. "It's a ghost," they said, and cried out in fear.

But Jesus immediately said to them: "Take courage! It is I. Don't be afraid."

"Lord, if it's you," Peter replied, "tell me to come to you on the water."

"Come," he said.

Then Peter got down out of the boat, walked on the water and came toward Jesus. But when he saw the wind, he was afraid and, beginning to sink, cried out, "Lord, save me!"

Immediately Jesus reached out his hand and caught him. "You of little faith," he said, "why did you doubt?"

And when they climbed into the boat, the wind died down. Then those who were in the boat worshiped him, saying, "Truly you are the Son of God." (Matt. 14:22-33)

Discussion

1. WHO ARE THE MAIN CHARACTERS?

    Jesus and Peter.

2. WHOSE FAITH WAS TESTED AND HOW?

    Peter's faith was tested. He wanted to walk on water, just as Jesus was doing. He started to walk but as the wind began to blow, he became fearful.

3. WHAT DID HE DO?

    He began to sink and cried out to Jesus for help.

    Trust in the LORD with all your heart and lean not on your own understanding; in all your ways acknowledge him, and he will make your paths straight. (Prov. 3:5-6)

4. WHAT WAS PETER'S CONSEQUENCE?

> Jesus held onto him and helped him into the boat. He then asked Peter why he doubted.

5. WHAT CAN WE LEARN FROM THIS SITUATION?

> Even when things look like they have taken a turn for the worse, Jesus is in control and there to hold our hands and help us if we fall.

> *Look at the birds of the air; they do not sow or reap or store away in barns, and yet your heavenly Father feeds them. Are you not much more valuable than they? (Matt. 6:26)*

6. WHY IS FAITH SO IMPORTANT TO GOD?

> Faith deals with believing something you can't see. So if you can't believe something in front of you that you can touch, you can't believe God, whom you can't see or touch.

> *And without faith it is impossible to please God, because anyone who comes to him must believe that he exists and that he rewards those who earnestly seek him. (Heb. 11:6)*

7. IS THERE A SUCH THING AS HAVING NO FAITH
AT ALL?

No. There are just different measures of faith. We all
have some measure of faith; we just operate on different
levels.

*We have different gifts, according to the grace given us. If a
man's gift is prophesying, let him use it in proportion to his
faith. (Rom. 12:6)*

8. HOW DO WE INCREASE OUR FAITH?

a. Hearing—Hearing the Word of God is more than just
going to church. We must intensively listen to what is
being taught as well as study at home on our own time.
We must then have an open ear and heart to hear what
God has to say to us.

*Consequently, faith comes from hearing the message, and the
message is heard through the word of Christ. (Rom. 10:17)*

b. Asking—Sometimes with God, it doesn't take much
work. We don't always need to beg, plead, cry, or
scream. Sometimes, all we have to do is ask.

*If any of you lacks wisdom, he should ask God, who gives
generously to all without finding fault, and it will be given to
him. But when he asks, he must believe and not doubt, because
he who doubts is like a wave of the sea, blown and tossed by
the wind. (James 1:5-6)*

c. Praying—Many people think that in order to speak to God we must do a thirty-day fast of only water in solitude. We can simply go into a private area of our choosing and speak to Him and believe that He hears us and will respond.

Therefore I tell you, whatever you ask for in prayer, believe that you have received it, and it will be yours. (Mark 11:24)

d. Speaking—The tongue is such a small part of our body but makes such a big difference. We must watch what we say because words have an impact, positively or negatively.

"I tell you the truth, if anyone says to this mountain, 'Go, throw yourself into the sea,' and does not doubt in his heart but believes that what he says will happen, it will be done for him. (Mark 11:23)

e. Our actions—Faith is more than just believing. We must do something about it. We must live by faith, knowing that with each step we take, God is with us, helping us to be more like Him.

We live by faith, not by sight. (2 Cor. 5:7)

Self-Reflection

1. When faced with a challenge, do I exhibit faith or fear?

2. Do I view things as the world views them, or do I see as God sees?

3. How often do I increase my faith by hearing the Word of God?

4. When things do not happen as fast as I'd like, do I stand on faith or do I take matters into my own hands?

5. How has faith changed my life? Can I imagine life without faith?

6. What can I do if I feel my faith decreasing?

7. If a word contrary to God's is spoken over my life, which do I believe? How do I respond?

Reference Scriptures

- *For by the grace given me I say to every one of you: Do not think of yourself more highly than you ought, but rather think of yourself with sober judgment, in accordance with the measure of faith God has given you. (Rom. 12:3)*

- *You see that a person is justified by what he does and not by faith alone. (James 2:24)*

- *And without faith it is impossible to please God, because anyone who comes to him must believe that he exists and that he rewards those who earnestly seek him. (Heb. 11:6)*

Life Application

The Bible tells us that if we have faith the size of a mustard seed, we can move mountains. I believe we are all born with an equal amount of faith. No one has more than anyone else. As life goes on, some people choose to work their faith, so it increases. Others choose to do nothing, so it decreases. Faith comes by hearing. Some people choose to speak life while others speak death. It's up to each person which to allow into the individual's spirit.

My spiritual father, Bishop Wayne T. Jackson of Impact Ministries International in Detroit, explains faith as a muscle. We were all born with equal amounts of muscle in our bodies. As babies, our muscles are not strong enough to do simple things like hold up the neck. But as time goes on, the muscles become stronger. Some people choose to exercise, so their muscles become even stronger and grow in size. Others decide not to exercise, so they are not as strong. That's how faith works: it's not enough to just have faith; we have to do something with the faith we have. If we say we have faith but do nothing with it, God can't get the glory, and we can't please God without faith.

Notes

~Chapter Seven~
OBEDIENCE

Obedience (noun)

A form of social influence in which a person yields to explicit instructions or orders from an authority figure.

For it is not those who hear the law who are righteous in God's sight, but it is those who obey the law who will be declared righteous. (Rom. 2:13)

Personal Encounter

Do you ever wonder why we do things we know we are not supposed to do, and then we try to justify it? I remember learning my first major lesson in obedience.

It was my sixth-grade summer vacation. We had recently moved to a new home, so I didn't know anyone in the neighborhood. All of my friends were in my old neighborhood, so I spent a lot of time at my grandmother's, who lived there. I was over there one day with my "boyfriend," my grandmother's next door neighbor, and my mom stopped by to take me home. My mom didn't particularly care for him so I was forbidden from seeing him.

When my mom came, she had my cousin with her so I would not be home alone. I remember thinking to myself, "No one is going to keep me from the one I love, not even you" (referring to my mother). So I decided to bend the truth. I was told I could not see my boyfriend, but not my grandmother, and I can go for a bike ride, can't I? I had figured out a loophole (I was very intelligent at a young age).

So the next morning I got up, packed us a lunch, ice water, and some money just in case, and told my cousin, "Let's go for a bike ride." She had no clue we were about to ride our bikes to my grandmother's house, about seven miles away. I knew it was a distance, but the ride in the car seemed so much shorter. And so we were off. Riding and laughing, laughing and riding, we were going to see my grandmother. That was my excuse, "my grandmother." The ride there was smooth. We had taken that route every day going to school, so I knew exactly where to go since I was very observant. We got there, spoke to everyone, including him, stayed for a little while, then we were off to go back home. (No one was going to keep me away, I was determined).

On the way back, I decided to take a different route. It was our alternative route to school. Why did I do that? There was an intersection that confused me. Instead of it crossing in a *T*, it crossed in an *X*. This took us out of the way about a mile and a half, but I still knew where I was going and how to get home. However, it started to get dark. Now no one knew where we were all day. They only knew we were going for a bike ride. By this time my mom was off work and I was starting to worry. What would she do to me if she found out I rode my bike all the way to my grandmother's house?

I was in trouble. The street lights were coming on by this time, and in my house, you better be on the porch when the street lights came on. I was really in trouble. We were still miles away from home, so I decided to take whatever was coming to me and call home. I didn't want to put my cousin in any more danger. So I stopped at a pay phone to call home. My mom knew exactly where we were so she told us to wait there until she came and got us. I had already started to cry because I just knew when she saw me it would be a disaster.

To my surprise, when she came, she gave us a hug, and put us in the car. My brother and his friend rode the bikes home and everything was okay. She told me I had punished myself enough so I wouldn't get reprimanded. She was right: I had learned a valuable lesson. When she says no, it's no. If I feel it's wrong, it's wrong. Year's later, we found out we stopped a block away from my cousin's father's house. So close and yet so far!

Occasionally we sit and laugh about this, but I could only imagine what I put my mother through. To come home and your young daughter and niece are nowhere to be found in a new neighborhood. I think now about children who did similar things and never came home, or came home different from the way they left. The heartbreak my family would have felt if something would have happened to me or my cousin—how could my mom explain that to my aunt? What would she say? How selfish that was for me to put us in harm's way to see a boy who had no clue of what I was doing? Was it worth it? I now know that God was definitely with us even before I came to know Him because who else could have covered and kept us? Praise be to my Savior!

Who Obeyed the Lord?

"I (Saul) *too was convinced that I ought to do all that was possible to oppose the name of Jesus of Nazareth. And that is just what I did in Jerusalem. On the authority of the chief priests I put many of the saints in prison, and when they were put to death, I cast my vote against them. Many a time I went from one synagogue to another to have them punished, and I tried to force them to blaspheme. In my obsession against them, I even went to foreign cities to persecute them.*

"On one of these journeys I was going to Damascus with the authority and commission of the chief priests. About noon, O king, as I was on the road, I saw a light from heaven, brighter than the sun, blazing around me and my companions. We all fell to the ground, and I heard a voice saying to me in Aramaic, 'Saul, Saul, why do you persecute me? It is hard for you to kick against the goads.'

"Then I asked, 'Who are you, Lord?'

"'I am Jesus, whom you are persecuting,' the Lord replied. 'Now get up and stand on your feet. I have appeared to you to appoint you as a servant and as a witness of what you have seen of me and what I will show you. I will rescue you from your own people and from the Gentiles. I am sending you to them to open their eyes and turn them from darkness to light, and from the power of Satan to God, so that they may receive forgiveness of sins and a place among those who are sanctified by faith in me.'

"So then, King Agrippa, I was not disobedient to the vision from heaven. First to those in Damascus, then to those in Jerusalem and in all Judea, and to the Gentiles also, I preached that they should repent and turn to God and prove their repentance by their deeds. (Acts 26:9-20)

But I have had God's help to this very day, and so I stand here and testify to small and great alike. I am saying nothing beyond what the prophets and Moses said would happen—that the Christ would suffer and, as the first to rise from the dead, would proclaim light to his own people and to the Gentiles." (Acts 26: 22-23)

Discussion

1. WHO IS THE MAIN CHARACTER?

   Saul (name changed to Paul).

2. WHAT WAS HE DOING IN JERUSALEM?

   He opposed the name of Jesus of Nazareth by persecuting the saints. He also tried to force them to blaspheme so they would be put to death.

3. WHAT WAS JESUS'S RESPONSE TO HIS ACTIONS?

   Jesus first asked Saul why he was persecuting Him. Jesus then told Saul to get up so that he may be appointed as a servant to spread the gospel and his testimony.

4. HOW DID HE REACT TO JESUS'S RESPONSE?

He obeyed the Lord and began to preach repentance, urging people to turn to God and prove their repentance by deeds.

5. WHAT WAS PAUL'S REWARD?

From that day on, God helped Paul to witness to large and small crowds about Jesus Christ.

6. WHAT CAN WE LEARN FROM THE SITUATION?

God chooses whom He wants to use, and we must be willing and obedient to His word. God can use anybody from any walk of life.

If you are willing and obedient, you will eat the best from the land; (Isa. 1:19)

Who Disobeyed the Lord?

S amuel said to Saul, "I am the one the LORD sent to anoint you king over his people Israel; so listen now to the message from the LORD. This is what the LORD Almighty says: 'I will punish the Amalekites for what they did to Israel when they waylaid them as they came up from Egypt. Now go, attack the Amalekites and totally destroy everything that belongs to them. Do not spare them; put to death men and women, children and infants, cattle and sheep, camels and donkeys.'"

So Saul summoned the men and mustered them at Telaim—two hundred thousand foot soldiers and ten thousand men from Judah. Saul went to the city of Amalek and set an ambush in the ravine. Then he said to the Kenites, "Go away, leave the Amalekites so that I do not destroy you along with them; for you showed kindness to all the Israelites when they came up out of Egypt." So the Kenites moved away from the Amalekites.

Then Saul attacked the Amalekites all the way from Havilah to Shur, to the east of Egypt. He took Agag king of the Amalekites alive, and all his people he totally destroyed with the sword. But Saul and the army spared Agag and the best of the sheep and cattle, the fat calves and lambs—everything that was good. These they were unwilling to destroy completely, but everything that was despised and weak they totally destroyed.

Then the word of the LORD came to Samuel: "I am grieved that I have made Saul king, because he has turned away from me and has not carried out my instructions." Samuel was troubled, and he cried out to the LORD all that night.

Early in the morning Samuel got up and went to meet Saul, but he was told, "Saul has gone to Carmel. There he has set up a monument in his own honor and has turned and gone on down to Gilgal."

When Samuel reached him, Saul said, "The LORD bless you! I have carried out the LORD's instructions."

But Samuel said, "What then is this bleating of sheep in my ears? What is this lowing of cattle that I hear?"

Saul answered, "The soldiers brought them from the Amalekites; they spared the best of the sheep and cattle to sacrifice to the LORD your God, but we totally destroyed the rest..." (1 Sam. 15:1-15)

The LORD said to Samuel, "How long will you mourn for Saul, since I have rejected him as king over Israel? Fill your horn with oil and be on your way; I am sending you to Jesse of Bethlehem. I have chosen one of his sons to be king." (1 Sam. 16:1)

Discussion

1. WHO WAS THE MAIN CHARACTER AND WHAT DID GOD TELL HIM TO DO?

   King Saul. God told him to attack the Amalekites and destroy *everything* that belongs to them.

2. WHAT DID HE DO INSTEAD?

   He attacked the Amalekites and totally destroyed everything that was weak. However, Saul kept Agag the king and everything that was good.

3. WHAT WAS SAUL'S CONSEQUENCE?

God was grieved that Saul did not follow out His instructions. God rejected Saul as king and replaced him with a son of Jesse.

But now your kingdom will not endure; the LORD has sought out a man after his own heart and appointed him leader of his people, because you have not kept the LORD's command." (1 Sam. 13:14)

4. WHAT CAN WE LEARN FROM THE SITUATION?

God will not accept anything. He wants our best and He wants us to be obedient to His word.

But Samuel replied: "Does the LORD delight in burnt offerings and sacrifices as much as in obeying the voice of the LORD? To obey is better than sacrifice, and to heed is better than the fat of rams. (1 Sam. 15:22)

5. WHAT ARE THE TERMS TO OBEDIENCE? (AS AN IF.....THEN...... STATEMENT)

a. If you serve God, then...

If they obey and serve him, they will spend the rest of their days in prosperity and their years in contentment. (Job 36:11)

b. If you do the will of God, then...

"Not everyone who says to me, 'Lord, Lord,' will enter the kingdom of heaven, but only he who does the will of my Father who is in heaven. (Matt. 7:21)

c.   If you love God, then…

Whoever has my commands and obeys them, he is the one who loves me. He who loves me will be loved by my Father, and I too will love him and show myself to him." (John 14:21)

d.   If you seek the Kingdom of God, then…

But seek first his kingdom and his righteousness, and all these things will be given to you as well. (Matt. 6:33)

e.   If you forsake God, then…

He went out to meet Asa and said to him, "Listen to me, Asa and all Judah and Benjamin. The LORD is with you when you are with him. If you seek him, he will be found by you, but if you forsake him, he will forsake you. (2 Chron. 15:2)

f.   If you disobey God, then…

If you do what is right, will you not be accepted? But if you do not do what is right, sin is crouching at your door; it desires to have you, but you must master it." (Gen. 4:7)

Self-Reflection

1. Has God ever called me to do something that I didn't want to do? Did I obey?

2. If not, did I try to justify my disobedience?

3. What am I willing to give up to obey God? Is it worth the price?

4. In which areas of my life do I have the most difficulty obeying God? Why?

5. How can I overcome that obstacle?

6. Do I believe living an obedient life hinders my relationships with others?

7. How do my peers feel about obeying God?

8. Besides God, whom else should I obey?

9. Is there ever a time when I should *not* obey God? If so when?

Reference Scriptures

- "Ask and it will be given to you; seek and you will find; knock and the door will be opened to you. For everyone who asks receives; he who seeks finds; and to him who knocks, the door will be opened. (Matt. 7:7-8)

- Delight yourself in the LORD and he will give you the desires of your heart. (Ps. 37:4)

- For whoever does the will of my Father in heaven is my brother and sister and mother." (Matt. 12:50)

Life Application

Here's the bottom line: God does not tell us what to do, He only tells us what will happen when we do it. The rest is up to us. It's our choice. No one else can make that decision. God gives us free will to do whatever we want, and we must accept responsibility for our actions. If we had no free will, there would be no test. That ultimately means there would be no testimony, so we would never see how awesome God truly is. How incredible is it that we have the ability to choose our own destiny each and every day we wake up in the morning. Not only that, but we have the ability to change ourselves so that our end result is acceptable and pleasing in God's sight. We don't have to be like our forefathers. We have the opportunity to be better than our forefathers. What a mighty God we serve!

Notes

Final Prayer

We all must sit and really ask ourselves: What do I want to be? Where do I want to go? How do I plan to get there? If your answer is "whatever God calls me to be, wherever God tells me to go, and however He chooses to get me there," then here a simple prayer to help you get there:

Heavenly Father, I thank you for creating me just the way I am. I thank you for calling me not just to be your servant but to be your friend. I ask you right now to order my steps according to your Word so that I may be acceptable and pleasing in your sight. Give me the wisdom to discern right from wrong, the power to choose right even when wrong is more tempting, and the strength to stand behind my decision even when it's not popular. Forgive me of my past mistakes, and help me to forgive myself. Help me to overcome my challenges so that I may help someone else who is going through the same thing. Guide and direct my path so that I can spread the gospel throughout all the nations, that not my will but your will shall be done. I thank you in advance for what you are about to do on my behalf. In the name of Jesus Christ I pray, Amen.